HISTORY UNCUT

THE REAL Marie Curie

Virginia Loh-Hagan

45th Parallel Press

Published in the United States of America by Cherry Lake Publishing
Ann Arbor, Michigan
www.cherrylakepublishing.com

Reading Adviser: Marla Conn MS, Ed., Literacy specialist, Read-Ability, Inc.
Book Designer: Felicia Macheske

Photo Credits: Bain News Service, Publisher, Library of Congress, Prints & Photographs Division, [reproduction number, e.g., LC-B2-1234], cover, 1, 5, 30; © Barabasa/Shutterstock.com, 7; © verbaska/Shutterstock.com, 9; © Dm_Cherry/Shutterstock.com, 11; © Glenkar/Shutterstock.com, 12; © Everett Historical/Shutterstock.com, 15; © Maksim Shmeljov/Shutterstock.com, 17; © IVASHstudio/Shutterstock.com, 19; © Oleg Golovnev/Shutterstock.com, 20; © GoodMood Photo/Shutterstock.com, 23; Pres. Warren G. Harding escorting Madame Curie down steps to south grounds of the White House. Washington D.C, None. [Between 1921 and 1923] Photograph. Retrieved from the Library of Congress, https://www.loc.gov/item/93512088/., 24; © zlikovec/Shutterstock.com, 27; © HUANG Zheng/Shutterstock.com, 29

Graphic Elements Throughout: © iulias/Shutterstock.com; © Thinglass/Shutterstock.com; © kzww/Shutterstock.com; © A_Lesik/Shutterstock.com; © MegaShabanov/Shutterstock.com; © Groundback Atelier/Shutterstock.com; © saki80/Shutterstock.com

45th Parallel Press is an imprint of Cherry Lake Publishing.

Library of Congress Cataloging-in-Publication Data

Names: Loh-Hagan, Virginia, author. | Loh-Hagan, Virginia. History uncut.
Title: The real Marie Curie / by Virginia Loh-Hagan.
Other titles: Marie Curie
Description: Ann Arbor, MI : Cherry Lake Publishing, [2018] | Series: History uncut | Audience: Grades 7 to 8 | Includes bibliographical references and index.
Identifiers: LCCN 2018004561| ISBN 9781534129559 (hardcover) | ISBN 9781534132757 (pbk.) | ISBN 9781534131255 (pdf) | ISBN 9781534134454 (hosted ebook)
Subjects: LCSH: Curie, Marie, 1867-1934—Juvenile literature. | Women chemists—Poland—Biography—Juvenile literature. | Women chemists—France—Biography—Juvenile literature. | Nobel Prize winners—Biography—Juvenile literature.
Classification: LCC QD22.C8 L644 2018 | DDC 540.92 [B] –dc23
LC record available at https://lccn.loc.gov/2018004561

Cherry Lake Publishing would like to acknowledge the work of The Partnership for 21st Century Skills. Please visit www.p21.org for more information.

Printed in the United States of America
Corporate Graphics

Table of Contents

CHAPTER 1

Marie Curie The Story You Know

Marie Curie was a scientist. She won 2 **Nobel Prizes**. She studied rays. She discovered 2 elements. One of them was **radium**. Curie said it was **radioactive**. It breaks down. It makes energy.

She helped develop **x-rays**. X-rays are special energy. They pass through things. They take pictures inside bodies. Curie helped during World War I. She helped doctors. She invented "Little Curies." These were special x-ray machines. The machines could move. They moved to hurt soldiers on battlefields.

Curie's work saved many lives. She paved the way for women in science. But there's more to her story...

Curie also invented special needles. The needles had radium gas. This cleaned rotting skin.

CHAPTER 2

Poor Little Marie

Marie Curie had a hard life. She was very poor. She was born on November 7, 1867. She was born in Warsaw. Warsaw is in Poland. Russia took over Poland. Curie's family didn't like that. They wanted Poland to be its own country. They lost their money. They lost their **property**. Property is land and things.

Curie's mother got sick. She died. Curie was only 10. She helped take care of the family.

She loved to learn. She was smart. Her father was a teacher. He gave her math problems. He brought home lab tools. Curie taught herself.

Curie also made money by cleaning glassware in labs.

Setting the World Stage

1867

- William F. Cody started hunting buffalo. He was called Buffalo Bill. He killed 4,280 buffalo. He did this in 17 months. He fed the workers of the Kansas Pacific Railroad. He was one of the most famous Americans at this time.
- The United States bought Alaska. The cost was $7.2 million. President Andrew Johnson signed the agreement. This purchase ended Russia's presence in North America. It gave the United States access to the northern Pacific area.
- In Sweden, Alfred Nobel invented dynamite. He sold it as "Nobel's Blasting Powder." Dynamite is safer than other explosives. It could be controlled. It changed how people built buildings. It changed how people fought in wars.

School costs money. Curie needed money. She worked. She was a nanny. She worked for a family. This family was related to her father. They were rich. Curie fell in love with the son. His parents rejected Curie. They thought she was too poor.

She saved money. She had an older sister. They made a deal. Curie paid for her sister's education. Then her sister paid for Curie's education.

Curie studied in Poland. Then she went to the University of Paris. She studied during the day. She worked at night. She was hungry a lot. She ate butter and bread. She drank tea.

She founded the Curie Institutes in Paris and in Warsaw. They are major centers of medical research.

CHAPTER 3

Secret School

Curie did well in elementary and high school. She was a top student. Her schools were for girls. Curie and her sister wanted more. They wanted to leave Poland. But they were poor. They weren't allowed to get higher education. The University of Warsaw was for men only. Russians had strict rules. Teaching women at the university was **illegal**. Illegal means not allowed. It was also illegal to teach Polish topics.

Curie and her sister found a way. They studied in secret. They went to the "Floating University." This was a secret Polish school. It was illegal.

The school was also known as the "Flying University."

Classes were held at night. They floated from place to place. Many took place at people's homes. Places changed all the time. Teachers and students hid. They hid from the Russians. Russians would have shut it down.

Polish teachers taught at the Floating University. They didn't like the Russian rules. They taught women. They taught men. They taught all topics. They taught science. They taught Polish history. They taught Polish culture. The school lasted 20 years.

Students gave a little money. They paid for the teachers. They paid for a secret library.

The Floating University served more than 5,000 Polish people.

All in the Family

The Curie family has won 5 Nobel Prizes. Marie Curie won 2. Her husband won 1. Her first daughter, Irène, won 1. Irène's husband won 1. Her second daughter, Eve, was the director of UNICEF when UNICEF won a Nobel Prize. Eve was a famous war reporter and author. She wrote a biography about Curie. Irène was a famous scientist. She continued to study radioactivity. She married Jean-Frédéric Joliot. Joliot was Marie Curie's assistant. Joliot and Irène had 2 children. Their names were Hélène and Pierre. Hélène is a nuclear physicist. Pierre's a biologist. He's a member of the French Academy of Sciences. Marie Curie came from a family of science lovers. Her grandfather taught physics and chemistry. Her father taught physics and math. Success and science run in the family.

"We must believe that we are gifted for something. And, that this thing must be attained." – Marie Curie

CHAPTER 4

Partner in Love and in the Lab

Curie finished school in Paris. She studied science. She studied math. She was ready to do research. She needed a place. But she had a hard time. People didn't support women in science.

In 1894, she met Pierre Curie. Pierre was also a scientist. He had a lab. He gave Curie room to work. He and Curie worked closely together. They fell in love.

He asked her to marry him. She said no. She wanted to go home. She returned to Poland. She couldn't get a job. The university wouldn't hire women. Curie returned to Paris.

Pierre studied crystals and magnets.

THAT Happened?!?

There's a famous photo of Marie Curie. It's shared online. It's even on postage stamps. But it's not Curie. It's a photo taken by Paul Schroder. It was taken in 2001. It was taken in his studio. Schroder wasn't tricking people. He was helping Susan Marie Frontczak. Frontczak is a professional storyteller. She plays famous women onstage. She pretends to be Curie. She's done this for more than 13 years. She's acted in more than 350 performances. She's performed in more than 30 U.S. states and 9 countries. The photo was meant to promote her own work. Frontczak has mixed feelings about the stamps. She's flattered that people thought she was really Curie. But she's not happy about her image being used without permission.

"Be less curious about people and more curious about ideas."

– Marie Curie

Marie and Pierre got married. They had 2 daughters. Curie loved them. But she also loved science. People were mean to her. They thought she should just be a mom.

Curie got a **doctorate**. She was the first woman in France to do so. Doctorates are the highest degrees. Pierre stopped his own work. He helped Curie.

In 1903, they won the Nobel Prize. People wanted to give it to Pierre only. Pierre fought back. He said it was Curie's idea. Curie was the first woman to win it. In 1911, she won another one. She was the first person to win 2 Nobel Prizes.

In 1906, Pierre died. Curie worked to stop feeling sad. She took over his teaching job. She taught at the University of Paris. She was the first woman to do so.

Pierre stepped into traffic. A carriage hit him.

CHAPTER 5

Fighting Back

Curie was a **widow**. Widows are wives whose husbands have died. Curie was still young. She fell in love with Paul Langevin. This happened in 1911.

Langevin was Pierre's student. He was 5 years younger. He was also married. He had 4 children. This caused a **scandal**. Scandals are events that upset people.

Curie had written love letters. Langevin's wife found the letters. She gave them to a newspaper. Newspapers printed the story. They weren't fair. They said mean things about Curie. They weren't as mean to Langevin. Women were treated differently.

Curie and Langevin didn't last. But Curie's granddaughter married Langevin's grandson.

She had planned to go to Sweden. She was going to accept her Nobel Prize. She was asked not to go. People were worried about the scandal. They blamed her. They judged her. They didn't want her there.

Albert Einstein was a famous scientist. He supported Curie. He told her to ignore the bad news. He told her to go. Curie listened to him. She went to Sweden. She accepted her award. She wouldn't be bullied.

She fought back. She said, "I believe there is no connection between my scientific work and the facts of private life."

Curie was sad about what was said about her.

Bad Blood

In 1911, Marie Curie wanted to join the French Academy of Sciences. This is an important group. It advises the government. It supports science. Curie competed against Edouard Branly. French newspapers wrote about them. Liberals sided with Curie. Conservatives sided with Branly. They said bad things about Curie. At that time, the Academy was all male. They rejected Curie. Branly won by 2 votes. An Academy member said, "Women cannot be part of the Institute of France." Branly was more French than Curie. He was more Catholic. And he was a male. He was an inventor, physicist, and professor. He helped invent wireless telegraphy. (It's like radio waves.) He was nominated for the Nobel Prize 3 times. He never won it.

"Nothing in life is to be feared. It is only to be understood. Now is the time to understand more so that we may fear less." – Marie Curie

CHAPTER 6

Money! Money! Money!

Curie didn't have a good lab. She used a shed. The shed was next to a science school. It didn't have a good air system. It was too hot or too cold. It had broken windows. It was leaky.

Curie wasn't rich. She gave away her money. She wanted to help the war effort. She tried to give away her Nobel Prize medals. The medals were gold. The bank wouldn't take them. So, she gave away her prize money.

Curie didn't make money from her discoveries. She shared her work. A small amount of radium was $100,000. She couldn't afford her own discovery!

People were surprised that the Curies did such great work under such poor conditions.

Curie needed more radium. She wanted to do more research. Missy Meloney was an American. She wrote for a newspaper. She helped Curie. She raised money. She created the Marie Curie Radium Fund. She told everyone Curie was a healer. She invited Curie to the United States. Curie did a tour. She did this in 1921. She spoke at many events. She hated talking in public. But she had to do it. She needed money. President Warren Harding invited her to the White House. He helped her. Curie made another trip to the United States in 1929.

Knowing President Harding helped Curie raise money.

CHAPTER 7

Death by Radium

Radium is dangerous. But the Curies didn't know this. Pierre kept some in his pocket. He showed off how it glowed. He showed off how it heated up. He had a **vial** of radium. Vials are small containers. Pierre strapped it to his arm. His arm was bare. He did this for 10 hours. His skin got burned. He didn't feel pain. He studied this.

Curie kept some at home. She kept it next to her bed. She used it as a nightlight. She carried some in her pocket. She said, "The glowing tubes looked like faint, fairy lights."

The Curies' lab notes are radioactive.
They are kept in a box lined with lead.

Explained by SCIENCE

Marie Curie loved Poland. In 1898, she discovered polonium. She named it after Poland. Polonium is a rare element. It's a silver powder. It's taken out of rocks with uranium. It's separated from radium. It can only be made in fancy labs. It's very dangerous. A small amount is deadly. Once polonium gets in the blood, it can't be stopped. It kills organs. It upsets stomachs. It causes hair loss. It's the perfect poison. It can't pass through skin, paper, or clothes. So, it can be hidden. It has no color or taste. It was used to poison Alexander Litvinenko. Litvinenko was a Russian spy. Polonium was put in his tea. He died 3 weeks later. Irène Curie was exposed to polonium. A container exploded in her lab. This may have led to her sickness.

"You cannot hope to build a better world without improving the individuals." —Marie Curie

The Curies touched radium all the time. Their lab notes are radioactive. So are their personal things. They're not safe to view. People must wear safety suits to see them.

The Curies didn't protect themselves. They got sick. They had pain. They felt tired. Their hands were shaky. Their fingers were cracked.

Curie died on July 4, 1934. She was almost blind. She had a blood sickness. She got it from radium. She got it from x-ray machines. She was exposed for a long time.

Scientists learned from Curie. They studied how radium affected humans. Even in death, Curie helped science!

Curie didn't blame radium for her sickness. She didn't know.

Timeline

1867 Curie was born. Her birth name was Manya Sklodowska. She was the youngest of 5 children.

1895 Curie got married. She wore a dark-blue dress. She also wore this dress in her lab.

1897 Curie gave birth to her daughter, Irène. Her father-in-law was a retired doctor. He helped take care of the baby. This allowed Curie to work.

1903 Curie earned a doctorate in physics. She studied radiation. Her professors said her work was a great contribution to science.

1903 The Curies were invited to the Royal Institution in London. Curie wasn't allowed to speak because she was a woman. Only Pierre could speak.

1904 Curie gave birth to her daughter, Eve. She hired Polish nannies. She wanted her daughters to speak Polish.

1906 Curie taught at the University of Paris. Hundreds of people lined up. They wanted to attend her first lecture.

1911 Curie went to Brussels. She attended the Solvay Conference. Only important scientists were invited. Curie was the only woman invited. She met Albert Einstein at this event.

1934 Curie died. She was buried next to Pierre.

1995 The Curies' bodies were moved. They were buried in the Panthéon. The Panthéon is in Paris. This is an honor. Curie was the first woman to be buried there for her own work.

Consider This!

Take a Position! Marie Curie said, "Radium was not to enrich anyone. Radium is an element. It belongs to the people." Curie shared her work. She didn't sell it. She didn't get a patent. Patents are official documents. They let people own an invention. They let people sell their inventions. Do you think Curie should have gotten a patent? Argue your point with reasons and evidence.

Say What? Marie Curie was a successful woman. She lived in a man's world. There weren't many women in science. Women weren't treated fairly. Explain Curie's struggles. Explain how she overcame these struggles.

Think About It! Learn more about radium. Make a list of the uses of radium. Make a list of the dangers of radium. How is radium beneficial? How is it harmful? Do you think radium is good or bad?

Learn More

Krull, Kathleen, and Boris Kulikov (illust.). *Marie Curie*. New York: Viking Children's Books, 2007.

O'Quinn, Amy M. *Marie Curie for Kids: Her Life and Scientific Discoveries, with 21 Activities and Experiments*. Chicago: Chicago Review Press, 2017.

Stine, Megan, and Ted Hammond (illust). *Who Was Marie Curie?* New York: Grosset & Dunlap, 2014.

Throp, Claire. *Marie Curie*. Chicago: Heinemann Raintree, 2016.

Glossary

doctorate (DOK-tur-it) the highest degree that can be earned from a university

illegal (ih-LEE-guhl) not allowed by law

Nobel Prizes (NO-behl PRIZE-ez) awards that go to people who do important work in science and art or toward peace; they are given out every year

property (PRAH-pur-tee) land and things you own

radioactive (ray-dee-oh-AK-tiv) the breaking down of atoms that produces energy

radium (RAY-dee-uhm) a scientific element

scandal (SKAN-duhl) an upsetting event that leads to gossip and rumors

vial (VYE-uhl) a small container

widow (WID-oh) a woman whose husband has died

x-rays (EKS-rayz) invisible and powerful beams of light that pass through skin and other materials; they let us take pictures inside bodies and other things

Index

About the Author

Dr. Virginia Loh-Hagan is an author, university professor, former classroom teacher, and curriculum designer. She would love to be part of a floating university. She lives in San Diego with her very tall husband and very naughty dogs.

GODS & GODDESSES OF THE ANCIENT WORLD

Odin

BY VIRGINIA LOH-HAGAN

Gods and goddesses were the main characters of myths. Myths are traditional stories from ancient cultures. Storytellers answered questions about the world by creating exciting explanations. People thought myths were true. Myths explained the unexplainable. They helped people make sense of human behavior and nature. Today, we use science to explain the world. But people still love myths. Myths may not be literally true. But they have meaning. They tell us something about our history and culture.

45th Parallel Press

Published in the United States of America by Cherry Lake Publishing
Ann Arbor, Michigan
www.cherrylakepublishing.com

Content Adviser: Alexandra Krasowski, Worcester Art Museum, Harvard University (Extension School)
Reading Adviser: Marla Conn MS, Ed., Literacy specialist, Read-Ability, Inc.
Book Design: Jen Wahi

Photo Credits: © Vuk Kostic/Shutterstock.com, 5, 15; © drumdredd777/Shutterstock.com, 6; © Bourbon-88/Shutterstock.com, 8; © alseeger/Pixabay.com, 11; © Forster Forest/Shutterstock.com, 13; © Mikhail Khromov/istockphoto.com, 19; © Derek R. Audette/ Shutterstock.com, 21; © Ezume Images/Shutterstock.com, 22; © Barandash Karandashich/Shutterstock.com, 25; © Drakuliren/ Shutterstock.com, 27; © Yosanon Y/Shutterstock.com, 29; © Howard David Johnson, 2018, Cover, 1, 17; Various art elements throughout, Shutterstock.com

45th Parallel Press is an imprint of Cherry Lake Publishing.

Library of Congress Cataloging-in-Publication Data

Names: Loh-Hagan, Virginia, author.
Title: Odin / by Virginia Loh-Hagan.
Description: Ann Arbor : Cherry Lake Publishing, 2018. | Series: Gods and goddesses of the ancient world | Includes bibliographical references and index.
Identifiers: LCCN 2018003331 | ISBN 9781534129412 (hardcover) | ISBN 9781534131118 (pdf) | ISBN 9781534132610 (pbk.) | ISBN 9781534134317 (hosted ebook)
Subjects: LCSH: Odin (Norse deity)—Juvenile literature.
Classification: LCC BL870.O3 L64 2018 | DDC 293/.2113—dc23
LC record available at https://lccn.loc.gov/2018003331

Printed in the United States of America
Corporate Graphics

ABOUT THE AUTHOR:

Dr. Virginia Loh-Hagan is an author, university professor, former classroom teacher, and curriculum designer. Like Odin, she has two wolves (untrained dogs) who follow her everywhere. Their names are Woody and Dotty. She lives in San Diego with her very tall husband and very naughty dogs. To learn more about her, visit www.virginialoh.com.